SHAWLS, CRINOLINES, FILIGREE

The author wearing an 1882 dress from her collection.

Shawls, Crinolines, Filigree

BY

CARMEN ESPINOSA

THE DRESS AND ADORNMENT

OF THE

WOMEN OF NEW MEXICO

1739 TO 1900

TEXAS WESTERN PRESS

THE UNIVERSITY OF TEXAS AT EL PASO

Library of Congress Catalog Card No. 72-138042

SBN 87404-026-4

TO MY MOTHER

RAFAELA MARTINEZ DE ESPINOSA

AND TO MY SISTERS

MARIA
[Mrs. J. J. Brazil]

IMELDA
[Mrs. Dennis Chavez]

ROSALINA
[Mrs. E. V. Kerr]

PEPITA
[Mrs. J. K. Blythe]

CONTENTS

❧ ILLUSTRATIONS ❧

The author wearing an 1894 dress (dark green satin with yellow roses).

[*Picture taken in 1947, Espinosa Collection*]

INTRODUCTION

MARIA DEL CARMEN GERTRUDIS ESPINOSA is uniquely quali-
fied to write a book on this rather specialized and predominantly
feminine topic — a history of Spanish fashions beginning in the
sixteenth century with emphasis on Spanish dress in New Mexico
in the eighteenth and nineteenth centuries.

By heritage and by chance, Carmen Espinosa has a deep-
rooted interest in her subject. She is a direct descendent of Mar-
celo de Espinosa, one of the captains who served with Juan de
Oñate, who established the first colony in New Mexico in 1598.

Born in Southern Colorado, Miss Espinosa attended schools
there and in New Mexico. In 1925, she attended the University
of Wisconsin, pledged Delta Delta Delta Sorority, and also
taught Spanish there. Later she continued studying and teaching
at the Universities of Oregon and Illinois. In the summer of 1930,
she studied in Spain at *El Colegio de los Pirineos* in Sarría, a
suburb of Barcelona. It was here that her interest in Spanish
fashions began, the result of her courses in Spanish history and art.

In 1935, Miss Espinosa returned to New Mexico to join the
staff of the Department of Education where she prepared art
and Spanish lessons for the rural schools of New Mexico. She was
Queen of the famous Santa Fe Fiesta in 1936. Her interest in
Spanish dress continued through the years. She wrote publications for the New Mexico department of education, articles for
the *New Mexico Magazine,* publicity for the annual Fiesta publications, and (in 1953 when the 200th anniversary of Albuquerque was celebrated) stories for the Albuquerque *Tribune.*

In addition, Miss Espinosa gave lectures on Spanish dress to
many organizations in Albuquerque, El Paso, and Tempe, Ari-
zona during the 1940's. She was on the list of lecturers on Inter-
American affairs during World War II.

While in Santa Fe, she began to read the books of early traders
who came to New Mexico after the American occupation of the
area. She was disturbed by the accounts which several of them

gave regarding the dress of the early women of New Mexico. It was then that the idea for this book came to her.

The research for her intensive study of Spanish fashions took her in several unexpected directions. For example, Miss Espinosa found much valuable information in the Santa Fe office of the Cadastral Engineer, an office which deals with the extent, value and ownership of New Mexico lands. Here she delved into the recorded wills of early New Mexico women. In these wills, she was surprised to find descriptions of many eighteenth and nineteenth century dresses (1714-1880), for these garments were so valuable that they were conveyed to heirs in the same way that land and property were bequeathed. Excerpts from several of these wills are included in this book to illustrate the detailed descriptions which the owners and lawyers gave the various dresses and items of jewelry.

In 1947, Miss Espinosa returned to Albuquerque, where she now lives. Her activities there have been varied. She painted the *reredos* in the University of New Mexico chapel, also the glass doors and windows in La Placita Restaurant in Old-Town. She worked for seven years in the office of her late brother-in-law, Senator Dennis Chavez. She has been active in the Albuquerque Historical Society, served as its president four years, and is now a board member. She is a member and former president of the New Mexico Folklore Society. At present, she is director of the Albuquerque Pan American Round Table.

Miss Espinosa has an extensive collection of Spanish dresses herself, several of which are modeled in the illustrations. She also has collected and made drawings of Spanish styles. In the Spring of 1970, she visited El Paso to make arrangements to publish the results of her years of work. The result is this book, which should be of interest to those who enjoy the beauty and elegance of a bygone age. Modes of dress reflect the mood and manners of the times. The Spanish fashions which Miss Espinosa discusses in text and photographs reveal a graciousness and femininity which obviously softened the harshness of the frontier life and brightened the bleakness of the Southwestern desert.

El Paso del Norte   CARL HERTZOG
June, 1970

Shawls, Crinolines,
Filigree

A BRIEF HISTORY OF SPANISH DRESS

৺ৄ AT THE BEGINNING of the sixteenth century, Spain was at the zenith of her power; her conquerors had carried her proud banner to the foremost confines of the known world; her King Charles I (1500-58) took the throne of Spain[1] to rule an empire unrivaled since the days of the Caesars. As the most powerful nation in Europe, Spain exerted powerful influence in customs, in dress, and in every phase of life. The Spanish infantryman, who knew no peer, was the example to be emulated as late as America's revolutionary times. The Spanish *peso* was the standard of exchange, as is the American dollar today. The dress of cultured Europeans of this period was rich and luxurious. Velvets, which had come into profuse use at the beginning of the century, were greatly improved in Spain, Italy, and Flanders.

In 1516, when Charles I became King of Spain, a cold, slender, grey-eyed youth, son of Joan the Mad (Juana la Loca) and of Philip the Handsome (Felipe el Hermoso) of Burgundy, and grandson of the Catholic rulers, Ferdinand and Isabella, great changes were brought about in the dress of the women of Spain. The court of Charles was the strictest and most punctilious in Europe. When the ladies of the court were informed that they could no longer bare their bosoms, they conformed to the edict by wearing plain or pleated chemises under their low cut bodices. In 1525, women wore the neck pieces higher and higher until 1530 when they surrounded their faces with broad embroidered ruffs with a narrow fluted ruffle. By the period of Felipe II (1556-1598), the ruffs had assumed such great proportions that spoons had to be designed with longer handles in order to take food to the mouth easier. These ruffs were worn by both men and

[1] In Spanish history Charles is also known as Carlos Quinto (Charles the Fifth), for he was Charles V of the Holy Roman empire. He became King of Spain (as Charles I) in 1516, was elected emperor in 1519, and was crowned at Aixla-Chapelle (modern Aachen) in 1520. He abdicated in 1556 and subsequently lived at the monastery of Yuste in Spain.

women. The first ones were called *lechuguillos*. When they became thicker, they were called *gorgueros*. The *gorgueros* were depicted by Domenico Theotokopoulos "El Greco" (1537-1614) in his portraits of the grandees of Toledo in the first half of the sixteenth century.

These neck pieces were followed in 1603 by the *golilla*, a plain, stiffened collar similar to those worn by the Puritans, except that the *golilla* was edged in lace. These neck pieces were worn by both males and females. A famous painting by Diego Rodriguez de Silva Velasquez (1599-1660) shows Philip V (1601-1665) of Spain wearing a *golilla*.

Immediately after the edict of Charles I, the well dressed Spanish women were wearing a creation of startling proportions, the *guardainfante* or *vertugadin*. Legend has it that this garment was designed for a Spanish queen to hide her state of pregnancy. In England it was known as the "farthingale." Thus the first crinoline was created, a garment whose place in history is most significant, for it continued in one form or another for years to come.

The *guardainfante* was worn over heavy garments, without a bodice, held by tape over the shoulders. A skirt was stretched over a framework of hoops and taped to create a smooth effect. Over this was worn a robe, beautifully embroidered in gold down the front, adorned with pearls and other jewels as befitted the wearer's station of life. A handsome girdle cord was tied at the waist, dangling almost to the feet. Over all this, an overdress opened down the front, showing the embroidered bodice and skirt of the underdress. The sleeves of this garment were of fine linen, tight fitting, ruffled and gathered in several places, then decorated with colored ribbons.

At the wrist was a gathered ruffle edged in fine lace, either gold or silver lace, or of fine linen thread. When the overdress had a sleeve, it was puffed at the shoulder and reached the elbow. This was cut in several pieces, the seams concealed by gold braid.

By the year 1550, the bodice was closed down the front and cut high until it reached the neck, with a high collar and frill. The bodice was cut broader, stiffened and padded. A corset of thin laths, two inches wide, held close by tape, was passed through the laths, giving the front a smooth appearance. The skirt was stretched from the hips on bell shaped, hooped petticoats. At court on important occasions, these gowns continued to be worn even after they were out of fashion.

In his *Historia del Toro en la Epoca Colonial (1520-1821)*, Nicolas Rangel of the *Academia de Historia Mexicana* describes the dress of the grandees who attended a reception given in honor of the new viceroy, El Marques de Villena, Duque de Escalona, Grandee of Spain. Translation from the Spanish:

On this event, the leading citizens wore breeches of plain red velvet with large slashes; the linings of the slashes were of orange or white silk; the sleeves of the blouses were also slashed. Some wore yellow silk stockings, others orange in contrast to the white ones of previous years. They wore black velvet capes and two colored plumes for ornaments; garters edged in gold lace were used by all.

The traffic on the streets on this occasion was so great that no carriages were permitted.

The ladies were not permitted to wear their *guardainfantes*. These hooped skirts had by this time assumed enormous proportions in the New World, emulating the dress of the women of the Mother Country.

The *guardainfantes* adorned the body of the Spanish woman as if she were an idol. All the gold and silver that had poured into Spain following the discovery of America and the Indies was heaped on the garments of women and men alike. This lavish display of gold and jewels seemed the best manner of showing the world the opulence of the wearer; also, it was the best way to safeguard valuables, for neither banks or safes existed at this time for the general public.

During the latter part of the sixteenth century, short coats of black silk were fashionable *(chamberlucos)*. Women's shoes were similar to those worn by men, except they were trimmed more elaborately. For outdoors, ladies wore thick soled shoes decorated with strips of colored leather, gilt buttons and other trimmings.

In headgear during the fifteenth and sixteenth centuries, women wore a headdress that covered most of the hair. This was close fitting about the face and decorated with pearls and jewels with a veil covering the nape of the neck. Later, they copied the low, small, cap-like hat of men, ornamented with gold cord and feathers. The middle class had an effective headgear style, a low, trimmed hat worn over a veil or hood. This form became very popular with the ladies in Italy. Since edicts were passed forbidding them to dress as did the upper classes, the lower class women wore no hats; they used small pieces of material to cover their heads or wore shawls. According to several writers, this was a heritage from the Moors who occupied Spain for seven centuries (8th through 15th) and with whom the Spanish were in continuous contact. To this day, the peasant women of Spain, despite their decorative costumes, seldom wear hats. They use mostly shawls or head coverings of silk and velvet.

The *guardainfante* continued to hold its place in fashion during the seventeenth century. This remarkable style spread to England and France, then to the Spanish colonial possessions and in a modified way to colonial America. It was revived in the United States during the Civil War period (1861-65). This style lingered in one form or another until the end of the nineteenth century.

In 1750 during the Rococo period, the Crinoline, a modified form of the *guardainfante,* was in full swing. Toward the end of the century, it was replaced by the "Polonaise,"[2] a bodice open in front, the skirt looped in the rear, showing elaborate underskirts. In the late nineteenth century following the period of the "directoire" styles, the crinoline was revived. The empress Eugenie Marie de Montijo (1826-1920), an aristocrat of Spanish lineage and wife of Napoleon III (1808-73), was an outstanding sponsor of this article of wear. She accompanied the Emperor on a tour of the Middle East in 1869, taking five hundred dresses with her. This was her way of showing the world the grandeur that was France; she called it her "political" wardrobe. The crinolines in her wearing apparel were numerous.

About 1870-75 came the *tournoure,* referring to the shape of the figure (plate 6). Finally, about 1882 came the bustle or the tilter (plate 7). This style had a sheaf of adornments to the rear — ruffles, laces and ribbons made like the over-decorated parlors of this period. In one form or another, the *guardainfante,*

2 "Polanaise," also a Polish dance.

the farthingale, the crinoline, the *tournoure,* and the bustle all had their beginning in the fashions of the women of Spain.

With the fall of Spain as a world power, her leadership in the world of fashion went into decline. France became the fashion leader and held this position of eminence until the twentieth century. Today, France is challenged by Italy, Spain, England, and the United States.

The Dress of New Mexico Women

During the nineteenth century, the women of New Mexico wore what the rest of the women of the civilized world were wearing, depending on their economic status in life.

In 1832, a trader named Josiah Gregg, a Missourian who engaged in trade from 1831 to 1840, came to New Mexico. Failing in health, Gregg had been advised to come west to recover his health. He made eight journeys over the Santa Fe trail and finally published his *Commerce of the Prairies* (1844). Gregg acquired a vast knowledge of the country, its physical features, natural resources, government, religion, crime and superstitions. He likewise wrote of the Indians of the Plains country. In one chapter, he writes of the dress of the women:

The Mexican woman is scarcely without her *rebozo* or shawl, except when laid aside for the dance. Indoors it is loosely thrown about her person, out of doors about her head. This garment affords a facility for the concealment of the person.

The normal apparel of the female peasantry is the *enaguas* or petticoat of home-made flannel of blue or scarlet cloth over a loose white chemise. It is even used by the ladies of rank.

I have observed among the upper classes, European dress is now frequently worn; although they are generally a year or two behind our latest fashions.

In 1850, William Watts Hart Davis came to Santa Fe, bearing an appointment as United States Attorney. He was a young man, a typical specimen of the Victorian American, confident of the superiority of the United States and the worth of Protestantism. Although New Mexico had been a part of the United States since 1846, the newcomers did not think of its people as citizens of the United States. The comments made by Davis regarding the dress of the New Mexican woman were similar to those of Gregg.

Of course many traders had come from the United States to New Mexico long before the territory belonged to this country. As early as 1804, the Mallert brothers came to Santa Fe. Shortly afterwards, Baptiste La Lande, a Creole trader from Louisiana, was sent by a Mr. Morrison of Kaskashia, Illinois. La Lande sold his wares at a high profit, remained in New Mexico, married a native woman and settled near Las Vegas, where his Lalandes descendants reside today.

In 1812, a party of St. Louis merchants under the leadership of a Mr. McKnight made their entry into New Mexico. The group was arrested as spies, their goods confiscated, then they were sent to Mexico City and later released. The same year, eighty traders from Missouri with a large train of wagons and other wheeled vehicles conveyed $30,000 worth of merchandise to Santa Fe.

The arrival of the caravans caused great excitement among the populace, who greeted the arrivals with shouts of, "Los carros! Aqui viene la caravana — los Americanos!" (The wagons! Here come the caravans — the Americans!)

However, except for the last group mentioned, most of the traders brought few supplies and it was not until the establishment of the Santa Fe Trail in 1822-24 that supplies in large quantities began to come into the province. The caravans were protected from marauders and Indians. Army troops accompanied the traders as far as the Arkansas river.

New Mexico was no longer a colony of Spain in 1822, for now it was part of the Republic of Mexico, since Mexico had declared its independence from Spain in that year. This separation was not deeply felt in New Mexico, for the area had been given scant attention by the Republic to the south. In 1846 when the United States took over New Mexico, the populace was in turmoil. Its citizens must cope with a different language, different customs and religion. Numerous misunderstandings resulted. The coming of the caravans along the Santa Fe trail occasioned a verse which was sung as follows: 'De Santa Fe a Franquilin, corren los Americanos; Robándoles el dinero, a todos los Mexicanos." (From Santa Fe to Franklin come the Americans, robbing the Mexicans of their money.)

Despite the misunderstandings, the traders were bringing and exchanging goods. They also brought the materials and merchandise which changed the fashions of women in New Mexico. No longer was the basic and primary influence Spanish. Traders from the South were replaced by traders from the East. Women's fashions ceased to be exclusively Spanish in design and style. Gradually they became modified by influences from the United States.

The era of the wagon trader was short lived, for by 1878, the Santa Re Railroad reached Raton, New Mexico. By July of the same year, it entered Las Vegas and in February, 1879, the short line to Lamy was established. In 1880, the line was extended to Albuquerque. Thus, after only fifty years of glory and hazards, the march of the Santa Fe trail was silenced forever by the steam power of the railroad.

And with the railroad came even more overpowering changes in the dress of New Mexican women. Lace *mantillas* were outnumbered by cotton bonnets and the *guardainfante* was replaced by the bustle.

Prominent Santa Fe family of the 1860's
Benigna Garcia de Delgado with daughters, Luz (standing) and
Marcella (with hat) and infant son, Emilio.

[Mrs. Delgado is the grandmother of Mrs. Frank V. Ortiz of Santa Fe]

⤛ THE WILLS ⤜

THE WILLS LISTED on the following pages were a challenge
and a game. At first glance the wording seemed difficult because
of the numerous abbreviations used, but as one read on, the reading became easier.

The spelling often is not modern. Many names of materials
and articles of wear required time and study before arriving at
their meaning.

The inks, surprisingly enduring have lasted through the years.
The early New Mexican probably availed himself of the earths
and plants in making the inks. The quill or other similar instru-
ment was used in writing. It is a matter of record that steel pens
were not used in New Mexico prior to 1846. Mr. Joab Houston,
Justice of the Territorial Supreme Court, named by General
Kearny at the time of American occupation, testified in a case
before the Surveyor General, where land grants were being
surveyed, that steel pens were unknown in New Mexico prior to
his coming to this region. He had been in the region long before
American occupation, presumably coming here with traders during the Santa Fe Trail days.

With American occupation, little or no attention was paid to
the archives. During the tenure of Governor William A. Pile
(1869-1871) the archives were distributed to the tradesmen in
Santa Fe to use for wrapping commodities because paper was
scarce. This lack of judgment came to the attention of an enter-
prising group, who demanded that such misuse of valuable pa-
pers be discontinued, which it was. Some of the Archives found
their way to private collections, some to the Huntington Library
and some to the Library of Congress. At the present time, the
majority are on microfilm at the Museum in Santa Fe.

Gowns and accessories listed must not be considered typical
of what the general public wore. The testators who made their
wills evidently were individuals of means and rank, as one can-
not testate if one has nothing to list. These wills provide the only

means of knowing what the early New Mexican woman wore before the coming of the traders and the Santa Fe Trail.

After trade was established, and after the 1880 arrival of the railroad, New Mexican women wore what the rest of the civilized world was wearing — styles being delayed and not changed with the seasons as now. The materials were of superior quality and lasted through many generations. The plates shown on pages 25-40, illustrate what many New Mexico women wore in the nineteenth century.

LIST OF WILLS EXAMINED

Archive No.	Year	Testator	Location
100	1704 Apr. 20	Marquez de la Nava Brasiñas Inventory of personal property and estate	Santa Fe
431	1712	Name defaced — information scant.	?
495	1714	Francisca de Misquia	La Cañada
680	1715	Gertrudes Martín	La Cañada
680	1715	María de Perea	Santa Fe
405	1725 Dec. 18	Name illegible — information scant	?
344	1727	Petronila Garzia — protesting division of goods and chattels of her deceased husband	?
406	1739 Oct. 25	Luisa Hurtado — (goods detailed later)	Santa Fe
530	1744	Margarita Martín — (goods Rio Arriba detailed later)	?
94	1746 Oct. 5	Josepha Baca	La Villa de Albuquerque
492	1749 Nov. 21	Fernando Padilla — complaint, having removed goods of his demented wife to her sister's house	La Villa de Albuquerque
513	1750 July 7	Ursula Chávez — claim for chattels given by her mother	?
93	1753	Juana Galván Coyota	?
552	1756	Juana Josefa Moreno	La Cañada
559	1763	María Gertrudis Martín	?
452	1765	María Manuela Lozano	?
48	1776	Gertrudis Armijo	Condado de Taos
626	1820	María Gertrudis Montoya	?
452	1830	Francisca Lobato	?
144	1831	Micaela Baca	Santa Fe

Imbentario de los bienes que quedaron con la muerte de Luisa Hurtado y tutela de sus hijos:

(Inventory of the goods left at the time of the death of Luisa Hurtado guardian of her children):

1 Pulsera de corales
   coral bracelet

1 Rosario de coral
   coral rosary

1 Santo de plata
   silver saint

1 Relicario de plata
   silver medallion

2 Anillos
   rings

2 Tumbagas
   rings of gold and copper

1 Mantón negro bordado con seda
   black shawl embroidered in silk

1 Mantón blanco bordado de escarlata con encajes guarnecidos
   white shawl embroidered in red and trimmed with lace

4 Platos de metal con un platón de lo mismo
   metal plates with one large tray of the same metal

4 Posuelos de china
   china bowls

1 Jarro de bapor
   vapor jug

1 Caldereta de calentar agua
   caldron for heating water

2 Cucháras de bronce
   bronze spoons

4 Sábanas de algodón
   cotton sheets

3 Sábanas de lana
   wool sheets

1 Espejo
   mirror

1 Santo Cristo de plata
   silver Christ

1 Mesa de bronce
   bronze table

10 Vacas grandes
    cows

6 Crías
   calves

1 Ternera de año
   yearlings

10 Ovejas
    sheep.

IMBENTARIOS DE LOS BIENES que quedan por fin y muerte de Margarita Martín, vecina que fué del Río Arriba jurisdicción de la Villa de Santa Cruz de la Cañada, partición y división de ellos entre hijos y herederos, como adentro se contiene, primeramente, unas casas de morada, sala, cocina, despensa, 2 dormitorios.

(Inventory of the goods that remained at the death of Margarita Martin, a resident of Rio Arriba, jurisdiction of the Villa de Santa Cruz de la Cañada, partition and division of them among the sons and heirs as hereby contained first of all, some dwellings, living room, kitchen, pantry and 2 bedrooms.)

Habaluada (Valued at)	Pesos	Habaluada (Valued at)	Pesos
2 Salas, 3 aposentos, 34 árboles frutales *2 living rooms, 3 rooms for storing grain, 34 fruit trees*	320	7 Hilos de perlas prietas *strings of black pearls*	160
1 Escaparate de madera torneado *cupboard lathe turned*	50	4 Baquetas *pelts — tanned*	85
		19½ Baras de sarga *yards of serge*	78
25 Vacas paridas a 25 pesos *cows with calves*	625	10 Baras de melendra negra *yards of rich black cloth*	100
19 Otras a 20 pesos *others*	380	10 Baras de punta de plata a 4 *yards of silver lace*	40
3 Toros bueyes a 20 pesos *bull oxen*	60	1 Tobadilla nueva con fleco de plata *a new skirt with silver fringe*	40
2 Bueyes capones a 25 *steer oxen*	50	1 Tobadilla usada *used skirt*	30
6 Becerros a 8 *calves*	48	1 Naguas de escarlata ya usadas *red used petticoat*	20
7 Caballos a 15 *horses*	105	1 Mangas de camisa perfiladas *drawn work sleeves*	22
304 Ganado menor a 2 *sheep*	608	1 Mantellina de razo azul, lampaza forrada en azul encarnada *blue silk damask cloak lined in red Chinese silk*	30
193 Crías de este año a 1 *yearlings*	193		

[continued on next page]

Habaluada (Valued at)		Pesos
	Unas Mangas de Bretaña para mujer, labradas con seda *British linen sleeves embroidered in silk, woman's*	10
	Una pollera saya de piquin morada *hoop skirt of pekin silk*	50
1	Manto de lustre con puntas *shawl with fringe*	40
1	Crucifijo de bronce *bronze crucifix*	25
2	Cuadrillos de Santa Isabel *paintings of Saint Isabel*	2
1	Tapapies de Capichola *ribbed silk skirt*	26
1	Acha *axe*	5
1	Escopeta *firearm, early Spanish, generally a flintlock*	3
1	Gurbia *curved tool*	3
2	Coas a 2 *hoeing sticks*	4
1	Cazo grande *large iron pot container*	12
1	Carreta *cart*	20
1	Carreta vieja *old cart*	12
1	Carretoncito *small cart*	15
1	Banca de Madera *wooden bench*	4
1	Mesa de pino *pine table*	6
1	Taburete de madera *wooden taboret*	1

Habaluada (Valued at)		Pesos
1	Caja de Michoacán, cerradura y llave *box from Michoacán, hinges and lock*	10
1	Cama alta de tabla con pilares *wooden high bed with pillars*	10
6	Platos de China — medianos a 3 *china plates medium size*	18
1	Jarro de cobre *copper jar*	6
1	Caballeriza de paja *thatched cattle enclosure*	22
1	Comal de fierro *skillet*	4
2	Sedazos con sus aros a 1 *sieves with their hoops*	2
1	Arpa de tañer *harp*	40
2	Metates de piedra a 2 *grinding stones*	4
2	Navajas de barba a 1 *razors*	2
	Tierras *lands*	470
	Tierras en San Gerónimo de Taos *lands in San Geronimo de Taos*	400
1	Yegua *mare*	15
2	Piezas de rescates *tracts of redeemed land*	200
	Otras de las mismas *others, same as above*	75
2	Chiquitas a 45 *small (plots of land)*	90
	Una yegua *mare*	20

TESTAMENTO DE JOSEPHA BACA, defunta vecina que fué de la jurisdicción de la Villa de Alburquerque y imbentario de sus bienes.

En este Puesto de San Ysidro de Pajarito en cinco días del mes de Octubre de 1746 años, y el Te-ente de Aldemor, Capp'n General de este Reynato, a los Capp Antt y Joseph Ortiz albaseas de Doña Josepha a cual el obedezerá y en esta conformidad pase a hacer los imbentarios y para que conste lo firmaron conmigo, los testigos de asistencia a falta de Escribano Publico y Real que no hay en este Reyno, doy fe —

Juan Moya (*rubrica*)   Geronimo A. Zeballos
                               Bernardo de Diego
                               basq. Borrego
                               Río Abajo

Antt: Ortiz (*rubrica*)

Quienentas cabezas de ganado menor.

Sien cabras — que componen número de 600 cabezas, los cuales tengo en poder de diferentes personas del Río Abajo.

Dos caballos, una escopeta con la funda.

Dos frenos, 7 pares de colleras, una carreta nueva.

4 cuartas — un rancho en San José de San Phillipe de Xmes.

2 achas — 3 cabadores.

Declaro tenerles pagado a los genízaros de Belem 17,750 adobes, apilados, y algunas bigas.

950 cabezas de ganado menor entre cuales hay 150 chicas, 32 vacas de vientre, 12 beserros de dos años, 17 beserros de naciencia.

Una caja con herraduras — un almires con mano.

Unas naguas de sarga viejas, otras nuevas, tres camisas, unas naguas blancas, medias, zapatos, cama con colchón, 3 sábanas, colchas, almuadas.

Declaro que a dos Yndias de my serbisio se pongan en plena libertad y que a cada una se le den 10 obejas. Idem declaro que como miserable y fragil pecadora tube seis hijos que son Antt Baca, Joseph Baca, Domingo, Manuel, Rosa y Isabel Baca, a los cuales crie, alimente, puse en estado y he dado con igualdad una parte de mis bienes.

Y también declaro por mis legítimos herederos a dos mis hijos los que repartan lo que quedare despues de sacados funerales y mandas y propicias.

[Translation on next page]

Last will and testament of Josepha Baca, defunct resident of the Jurisdiction of the Village of Albuquerque, and inventory of her goods.

In this Hacienda of San Ysidro de Pajarito on the 5th day of October, 1746, Ten-ente de Aldemor, Captain General of this Kingdom, to Captains Antonio and Jose Ortiz, Executors of Doña Josepha, who shall obey, and to which he will comply and conform therewith and proceed to make inventory (of the estate) and in witness thereof this is signed by the assisting witnesses, for lack of a Public Royal Scrivner.

Juan Moya (*rubrica*)   Signed,

                                    Geronimo A. Zeballos   basq. Borrego
                                    Bernardo de Diego   Río Abajo

Antt: Ortiz (*rubrica*)

Five hundred head of sheep.

One hundred goats, which make 600 head that I have in the hands of different people of Río Abajo.

Two horses, a musket with its case.

Two bridles, seven pairs horse collars, a new cart.

4 whips — a ranch in San Jose de San Phillipe de Xmes.

2 axes, 3 hoes.

I declare to have paid to the Genizaros of Belen, 17,750 adobes, piled, and some vigas.

950 head of sheep, among which are 150 lambs, also 32 milk cows, 12 yearlings 2 years old, 17 new born calves.

A chest with its iron work. A mortar and pestle.

Some old serge skirts, others new, three blouses, white skirts, stockings, shoes. A bed with its mattress, 3 sheets, bedspreads and pillows.

I declare that two Indian women, whom I have in my service shall be given their freedom, and ten sheep to each of them.

I also declare that as a miserable and weak sinner I had six children who are Antonio Baca, Joseph Baca, Domingo, Manuel, Rosa and Isabel Baca, whom I brought up, fed and had married, and I have given them an equal part of my possessions.

I also declare as my legitimate heirs, two of my sons, who shall divide what is left after the funeral expenses, masses and alms.

EL SIETE DIAS DEL MES DE MAYO del año 1753, Juana Galvana Coyota.

(7th day of the month of May, the year 1753, Juana Galvana Coyota.)

333 Cabezas de cabras, carneros, padres, obejas
heads of goats rams and ewes

6 Bueyes
oxen

42 Vacas
cows

28 Becerros
calves

3 Toros
bulls

41 Yeguas y caballos
mares and horses

1 Mula
mule

1 Macho
mule

4 Mantones, 2 pintados, uno bordado
4 shawls, 2 painted, 1 embroidered

1 Cobija de escarlata
red cloak

1 Cobija de tafetan
taffeta cloak

2 Relicarios de plata
silver medallions

1 Santo Cristo de metal
metal holy Christ

6 Santos
saints

1 Colcha camera
bed cover

1 Fresada
wool blanket

1 Cuero de cíbolo
buffalo skin

Unos zapatos de uso
some shoes

1 Mantón negro
black shawl

1 Mantón blanco
white shawl

Condado de Taos — Año 1776

Manuel Vigil, Alcalde del Pueblo de San Gerónimo de Taos, cumpliendo con mando del Governador y Capitán General, Don Fermín de Mendinueta, por estas, doy cuenta y reporte de los bienes que según mimemoria mi esposa trajo al tiempo de nuestro matrimonio, como sigue:

Cien vacas de todas edades

400 ovejas

300 pesos, en plata

Una fragua

Un yunque

Un tornillo y martillo

303 pesos en cambio menor que se me deben por los 200 soldados de éste Real Presidio de Nuevo Mexico

 16 cueros (de cinco ases de tapuya)

 56 cabezas de ganado mayor de las tierras arribas

 15 caballos

300 mulas y cuatro otras con sus aparados

122 que fueron usadas en Chihuahua como me recuerdo. Un rancho que compre en venta real, situada en Piedra Negra de Taos.

560 reces que me costaron trecientos cincuenta pesos para herrarlas

550 ovejas que tenía dadas a partido. Estas ovejas han sido matadas por los Navajoes. Solamente he recibido 77 de éstos con lo cual quedo satisfecho

  2 pares de tenazas

300 cueros curtidos

300 pesos en cambio menor

La ropa que queda de mi finada esposa como sigue:

  1 enagua de seda con punta de plata y fleco hecho a mano

  2 kimonos del Japón

  1 enagua de paño

  1 capa corta de terciopelo   *(firmado)* Manuel Vigil

[continued on next page]

Recuerdo haber traído a nuestro matrimonio los siguientes bienes, obtenido de mi finado padre:

200 ovejas

12 caballos
Una mula y un macho

12 pinturas en lienzo, otras 12, 24 por todo, cada una bara en altura

1 docena de platos de peltre

1 docena de tazas de china

2 cajas de Michoacán (cada con su equipaje)

equipaje de cocina (para agua)

una casuela de hierro, con su cuchára

enagua de capichola, sin adorno, otra con hilo de oro

otros trajes finos y una capa con una pollera

2 trajes de lana de castilla, cada con capa, saco y calcones y una capa con pollera.

[Translation]

Archive No. 48   THE WILL OF GERTRUDIS ARMIJO

County of Taos — Year 1776

Manuel Vigil, Alcalde Mayor of the Pueblo of San Geronimo, fulfilling an order made by Governor and Capitan General, Don Pedro Fermín de Mendinueta, I hereby make this account and report of the possessions which I recall that my wife brought at the time of our marriage, as follows:

About 100 head of cattle, all ages

400 sheep

300 pesos in silver
a blacksmith shop, an anvil, a vise, a hammer

303 pesos in small change which are owed me by 200 soldiers of this royal presidio of New Mexico

16 pelts (de cinco ases de tapuya)

~~~~~~

{ 18 }

56 head of cattle from the upper lands

15 horses

300 mules and 4 other mules (aperados)

122 that were used in Chihuahua, which I still recall to mind. A ranch which I purchased at a Royal Sale, situated in Piedra Negra de Taos.

560 head of cattle which cost me three hundred and fifty pesos to brand

550 sheep which I had out on shares

My above mentioned sheep have been killed by the Navajos. I have received only 77 of these, with which I am satisfied.

2 pair of pliers

300 tanned pelts

300 pesos in small change

The existing garments of my late wife are as follows:

1 skirt of ribbed silk with silver braid and hand made fringe

2 Japanese kimonas

1 cloth skirt

1 short velvet cape.

(Signed) Manuel Vigil

The following I recall as having brought to my marriage, this acquired by my late father:

200 sheep

12 horses

A mule and a he mule

12 paintings on canvas, another 12, 24 in all each a (bara) high

1 dozen pewter plates

1 dozen china cups

2 chests from Michoacán (with their equipment)

Kitchen equipment (for water)

Iron kettle

Iron skillet with iron spoon

A skirt of ribbed silk, plain, another with gold thread

Other fine garments, a cape and a hooped skirt.

2 suits woolen castille cloth, with cape, waist coat and trousers

Condado de Santa Fe — Año de 1785

DECLARO TENER MIS ARMAS de escopeta, lanza, cartuchera, silla y fre-no, cofrenillas. Es my voluntad sea pa mi hijo el maior de este seg-do matrimonio:

3 cajas viejas, dos con cerraduras
1 solapa azul mui bieja
1 chupa de uniforme — otra blanca
1 capa sin forro
1 fusil de armamentos
1 pistola
1 lanza de Espanya
    Unas bolsas con su parmiel de baqueta y bocal de fierro

1 navaja bieja
1 par de espuelas y unos botines biejos
1 freno
1 silla y estribos de palo
1 cofrenillo mui biejo
1 ymagen de un crucifijo con la Dolorosa al pie de metal
3 estamps biejas.

[Translation]

I DECLARE *my arms, lance, cartridge pouch, saddle and small locker. It is my wish that these be for my son, the eldest of this second marriage.*

3 old chests with locks
1 very old blue waistcoat
1 jacket for a uniform, another white one
1 unlined cape
1 flint-lock musket
1 pistol
1 lance from Spain
    Some pouches trimmed in leather with iron rings for openings

1 old knife
1 pair of spurs and a pair of old leggings
1 bridle
1 saddle with stirrups of wood
1 very old locker, a small one
1 image of a crucifix with Our Lady of Sorrows, at the foot, of metal
3 very old prints

(conclusion missing)

2 Polleras, una de lana amarilla, una de piquin
   hooped skirts, one of yellow wool, the other of Pequin silk

1 Tapapies de razo verde
   overshirt of green satin

1 Tapapies de razo encarnado, aforado en mitan anteado
   overshirt of red satin, lined in yellow-colored lining

1 Paño de tela encarnada
   dress length of red material

1 Manto con puntas
   shawl with fringe

1 Chamberluco negro de capichola con fleco negro y blanco, guarnecido
   con argenteria de plata
   short, ribbed silk jacket, with black and white fringe, trimmed with silver lace

Unas pulseras de corales
   coral bracelets

Medias de seda encarnadas
   red silk stockings

Caxa de polvos, de moncorneo con el se seguillo de plata
   powder box with silver lock

1 Sortija de oro con tres piedras
   gold ring with three stones
	1 Quarta larga
	   long whip

3 Anillos de plata
   three silver rings
	3 Camisas
	   blouses

1 Baulito de caray
   small tortoise shell chest
	3 Naguas de escarlata
	   red skirts

3 Faldillas de manta de algodón, usadas
   petticoats of coarse cotton — used

1 Tapapies de sarga verde, otro de paño con fleco de listón amarillo
   a green serge skirt, another of blue material with yellow ribbon fringe

Encaje teñido amarillo
   yellow dyed lace

Caja de polvos dorada de golpe
   a powder box of hammered gold

1 Cofrecito de tabaco guarnecido de fierro
   a small tobacco box, adorned with iron work

12 Cucharas de plata
   silver spoons

(remainder of will missing)

Santa Fe — 6 de Agosto de 1831

Declaro mis bienes las casas de mi morada que se compone de 8 piezes, medio corral, media guerta y portales, un rancho en el Valle de Taos — 1000 obejas, que se hallan a partide en — Pedro José Perea.

I declare my property, dwellings which are composed of 8 rooms, a small corral, a small vegetable garden and porches, a ranch in Taos Valley, 1000 head of sheep, which have been consigned on shares to Pedro José Perea.

3 Cajones
chests

1 Caja era de mi madre — que se venda por misas por el bien de su alma
chest that was my mother's — let it be sold and the amount be used to pay for masses for the repose of her soul

1 Túnico de raza, nacar
silk cream dress

1 Azul de saya saya
blue Chinese silk

1 De ninfa
of gauze

1 Mantón
shawl

1 Cazo
large pot

1 Cazuela
small pot

5 Cubiertos de plata
silver plates

1 Tembladera
silver bowl

Todo ésto que anoto en esta cláusula fue adquerido en my primer nuncia, lo que se reparta como corresponda.

Idem declaro:

All that I list in this clause was acquired during my first marriage, let it be distributed to whom it corresponds.

I declare:

1 Mantón negro
black shawl

Chales de Seda
silk shawls

1 Túnico de moselina bordado
a muslin embroidered dress

1 Túnico de regilla
dress of thin muslin

[continued on next page]

1 Túnico de moselina con olan
dress of muslin with ruffle

1 Capichola negra
black ribbed silk

1 Par de aretes de oro
pair of gold earrings

2 Hilos de cuentas de oro, redondas
strings of round gold beads

3 anillos de oro
gold rings

4 Túnicos de indiana
cotton dresses

4 Sábanas
sheets

3 Colchas — 2 de algodón, 1 de lana
3 bed spreads, 2 cotton, 1 wool

2 Fresadas altimas
native wool blankets

2 Americanas
american blankets

9 Colchas de lana
woolen blankets

2 Colchas de algodón
cotton blankets

Una de las dichas colchas mando se den a mi muchachito Juan. A mis dos criadas 1 colcha y sábana de manta y a mi Jesus una fresada azul nueva.

Let one of the above mentioned blankets be given to my boy Juan. To my two servants, 1 blanket and cotton sheet. To my Jesus, a new blue wool blanket.

2 Almarios con llabe
cabinets with keys

1 Baul forrado en anta
trunk lined in elk skin

2 Baules forrados Mexicanos
lined Mexican trunks

3 platos de china
china plates

4 Espejos chicos
small mirrors

4 Espejos grandes
large mirrors

ARTICLES OF WEAR LISTED IN THE WILLS

Mantones or Mantas — *shawls*
Mantilla de seda — *silk mantilla*
Mantilla de encaje — *lace mantilla*
Chamberluco — *fitted short jacket*
Pollera — *hooped skirt*
Mantelina — *cloak*
Medias de seda — *silk stockings*
Petas — *corselets*
Paño de toca — *veil for head dress*

Quimones — *japanese cotton printed robe*
Dengue — *short cape, elbow length*
Camisas — *blouses*
Tapapie — *rich, silk decorated skirts*
Tobadilla — *rich skirt*
Fadillas — *petticoats*
Faldas — *skirts*
Chales — *shawls*

FAVORED COLORS for the elaborate, rich skirts above mentioned, are:

Negro — *black*
Azul — *blue*
Escarlata — *red*
Morado — *mulberry*

Nacar — *ivory*
Color de Arena — *sand color (beige)*
Sangre de Toro — *bulls blood (maroon)*

MATERIALS LISTED IN THE WILLS

Melendra — *a heavy silk*
Lampaza — *figured silk*
Saya Saya — *Chinese silk*
Capichola — *ribbed silk*
Lino de Bretaña — *British linen*
Gaza — *silk gauze (chiffon)*
Gaza labrada — *figured gauze*
Gaza de hilo — *Cotton gauze*
Razo — *Satin*
Manta — *coarse cotton cloth*
Sarga — *Serge*

Mitan — *lining material*
Seda bordada — *embroidered silk*
Ninfa — *thin chiffon*
Escarlata — *Native dyed red cotton*
Seda muare — *moire silk*
Indiana — *cotton print*
Seda Damaska — *silk damask*
Regilla — *buckram*
Moselina — *muslin*
Terciopelo — *velvet*
Tafetan — *taffeta*

TRIMMINGS

Punto de oro — *gold lace*
Punto de plata — *silver lace*
Fleco de oro — *gold fringe*

Fleco de listón — *ribbon fringe*
Listón labrado — *embossed ribbon*
Chaquira — *bead trimming.*

PLATE 1 — *Mantón de Manila*

Black crepe with colored flowers and fauna. Purchased in
Sevilla, Spain, 1930, Calle de las Sierpes (old when bought).

[Carmen Espinosa Collection]

PLATE 2 — *Mantilla, Black Blonda Lace*
From a painting of the author at University of Illinois, 1928.
[*Carmen Espinosa Collection*]

PLATE 3 — *Mantilla, grey and white, Blonda lace*

[Courtesy Cecily Bryan Kerr, Washington]

PLATE 4 — *Mantón de Manila*

Purchased in California, 1840, by prominent merchant of Valencia County,
New Mexico, Boleslo Romero. The model, Felice Gonzalez,
is the fifth generation to wear this Mantón.

PLATE 5 — *Mantilla of Chantilly Lace*
(Over 100 years old).

[*Carmen Espinosa Collection — see page 42*]

PLATE 6 — *Visiting Dress 1871*

Frances Delgado Espinosa wearing her mother's dress, beige taffeta with fringe. Carriage parasol, black, 1860.

PLATE 7 — *The Tilter or Bustle of 1880*
From the trousseau of Rosa Davila de Romero.

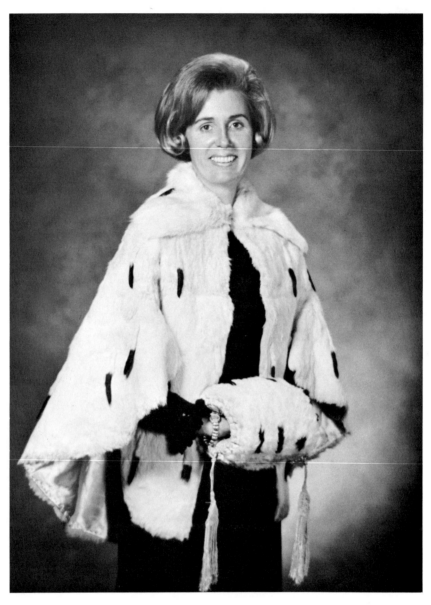

PLATE 8 — *Ermine Cape and Muff*

*Purchased by the author's grandfather, Captain Julian Espinosa, U.S.A.,
for his daughter Sofia, 1864.*

[Courtesy of Captain Espinosa's granddaughter, Mrs. Placida Garcia Smith, Phoenix]

PLATE 9 — *Wedding Dress of 1880*
Modeled for the Historical Society Fashion Show in 1953.
[*Courtesy of Mrs. William Nabor of Albuquerque, granddaughter of the original owner*]

PLATE 10 — *Wedding Dress*

Sofia Espinosa (author's aunt) married to Amarante Garcia, 1882,
El Carnero, Colorado.

PLATE 11 — *Wedding Dress of 1882*
Rosa Davila de Romero, Valencia, New Mexico, married to Andres Romero.
[Courtesy of Mrs. Max Gonzalez, granddaughter]

PLATE 12 — *Mantón de Manila*
Circa 1850.
[Tortoise shell comb and Mantón, courtesy of Mrs. Adelina Ortiz Hill]

PLATE 13 — *Costume for Santa Fe Fiesta*
This picture, taken in 1955, shows the author modeling her
1936 Fiesta Queen dress.

PLATE 14 — *Mantelina of 1895*
Black Taffeta trimmed with Chaquira
[Courtesy of Betty Pilkington]
[Parasol 1860 — Carmen Espinosa Collection]

PLATE 15 — *Peineta, heirloom of tortoise shell*
[*Courtesy of Consuelo Chavez, Santa Fe*]

PLATE 16 — *Mantón de Manila*

Purplish blue background with white embroidery.

[Circa 1840, courtesy Mrs. W. E. Blythe, Albuquerque]
[Shell comb — Espinosa Collection]

EL MANTON DE MANILA
The Shawls from Manila

⌘ THIS EMBROIDERED, SILK CREPE SHAWL, originally a product of China, was imported to Spain from Manila. It is no longer plentiful, although the shops in Spain and Mexico may have limited stocks. In 1930, while a student in Spain, the author purchased one in a shop en la Calle de las Sierpes in Sevilla, which had mantones of all colors. The stacks then were numerous. The history of this article of wear and adornment is most interesting.

Its discovery goes back to March 16, 1521, when Ferdinand Magellan, a Portuguese navigator in the employ of the Spanish government, arrived at exotic islands in the Pacific. He named them *Islas de San Lázaro* as they were reached on that Saint's day.

Four expeditions were made to these islands through the years that followed. These were led by García Jofre López de Loaïsa, Alvaro de Saavedra and Ruíz López de Villalobos. By the year 1600, the entire archipelago was in the possession of the Spaniards, and they were renamed *Las Islas Filipinas* in honor of the crown prince who later became Felipe II.

Now began extensive trade with the Orient, goods being transported by the Manila galleons to the port of Acapulco and other ports, thence to Spain. Among the many articles and goods exported were the *Mantones de Manila.* The women of Spain and of its possessions became so enamored with this article of wear that it was adopted as part of their wardrobe. For many years this *mantón* was known as the Spanish Shawl. These shawls were embroidered by men, on large frames, two men working simultaneously on either side, using fine ivory needles. Thus the embroidered fauna of the countryside, birds and floral effects are the same on both sides. The silk fringe was added later. Those of very delicate and fine embroidery are the oldest. About 1830 the shawls with the huge floral effects came into vogue.

These mantones come in diverse colors, also white and silk

crepe, with multi-colored flowers, birds and fauna most prevalent. Plate No. 16 shows a purplish-blue embroidered entirely in white. Plate No. 1 shows one with black background with flowers and leaves in shades of red and green. Plate No. 4 is lemon colored with floral effects in various pastel shades.

These shawls were produced in China primarily for export; however, since China has found in embroidery one of its most artistic expressions, these may have been used there too. For centuries China produced elaborate and delicate embroidery in wall hangings, dress and other articles. From the Chinese the intricate and colorful embroidery of the China Poblana dress of Mexico was adopted.

Numerous mantones are listed in the wills which have been recorded here, and to this day, *Mantones de Manila* are to be found in many homes of New Mexico women of Spanish ancestry and in the homes of those who have traveled to the Orient. Today they are treasured more than ever, for they are no longer manufactured.

Many Spanish painters have gloried in depicting this handsome adornment, among them Ignacio Zuloaga, Rodríguez Acosta, Carlos Vásquez, Llaseras and others.

LA MANTILLA

The Lace Head-Covering

THIS ACCESSORY to the attire of the Spanish woman merits special attention. The lace scarf held up by the tall comb enhances any face, be it one of beauty or not.

Lace has been used in Spain as an adornment since the earliest days. When Spain was at her zenith, Flanders and Belgium, having moved into a leading position in the development of handmade lace, supplied Spain with lace mantillas. Lace of gold and silver have been produced in Spain for years, used mainly by the clergy for altar decorations and by royalty and individuals of rank for dress and adornment.

At the beginning of the eighteenth century, many lace factories were established in the cities of Catalina, Amagro en La Mancha and Castilla La Vieja.

To this day, Barcelona, Talavera de la Reyna, Valencia and Sevilla are the centers of this art. Squares of velvet or silk edged in gold and silver lace were generally used as head covering since earliest days. These were the forerunners of the mantilla.

The mantilla as a head dress came into vogue about 1700. This article of wear was *de rigeur* at Court and a symbol of gaiety at fiestas and weddings.

France manufactured laces of many types, a favorite for the Spanish mantillas was the lace made at Chantilly. When Louis XIV married María Teresa, a daughter of King Phillip IV of Spain, the Spaniards were impressed by the extravagant use of lace in France and began making laces of silk and cotton. In the *point d'Espague* lace, Spain displayed her characteristic genius, influenced by the intricacies of Moorish art.

When reading the wills of the 1700's, the author questioned the head dress of the ladies. However, after reading volumes on the History of Spanish Dress, she realized that the women of the Provinces and ladies of rank have covered their heads throughout the ages on all occasions, either with silk or velvet scarfs, plain black or white materials, and after 1700, with lace mantillas. In the volume already cited, *Historia del Toreo en México*, mention is made of the mantilla around 1700.

Madame Calderón de la Barca, the English wife of the Spanish Ambassador in México, mentions the *mantillas* worn by the Mexican women in her volume entitled *Life in México* (1842). She also mentions the extensive use of *Blonda* lace as a dress decoration. *Blonda* lace is another popular type used in mantillas.

In the making of the finest silk lace mantillas, raw silk is used. This becomes ivory in color as it ages. Never fold a mantilla when putting it away, for the silk will split with age. Simply crush it and place it in a cloth bag.

As in the case of the *Mantones de Manila,* many painters have depicted the *mantilla* in their art: Ignacio Zuloaga, J. Llaseras, Manuel Benedito, and others. As with the *Mantones de Manila,* women of New Mexico cherish this article of wear as it is handed down from generation to generation.

EL TÁPALO
The Shawl

⁓§ THIS GARMENT was widely worn by New Mexican women in the 1800's and early 1900's. Now it is a thing of the past. It was worn mostly by women in the villages and especially at funerals. The city ladies scorned this article.

This shawl of fine wool chambray edged in silk fringe (the deeper the fringe, the more expensive the garment) covered the head and body completely. Thus the wearer did not have to give too much attention to her wearing apparel when going to early mass or to town. It was thrown over the shoulder and across the face, at times leaving only the eyes to be seen. At funerals it was a must, a requisite for older women, and at times worn even by the younger.

In the wills of early days these are called *mantas*. It is not known where the word *tápalo* originated. Its meaning is "cover it." It really covers the body from head to ankle.

Today the young girls of Andalucía, Spain wear them draped tightly about their shoulders, leaving the head uncovered and the tall shell comb much in evidence. In some provinces the older women cover their bodies completely as did the New Mexicans. They are called *tapadas*, covered ones.

The *manta* has been used in Spain for at least five centuries, utilizing materials of all sorts. It seems to be a heritage from the days of the Moorish occupation, when women's heads were covered.

LA PEINETA
The Comb

⁓§ THE TALL TORTOISE SHELL *peineta* is essentially a purely Spanish feminine adornment. This came into general use when the mantilla became popular, thus displaying the fine laces with grace and elegance. Combs of all kinds have been popular even before the mantilla came into use, combs of metal, ivory, gold or silver. In the colonies the latter were very popular, even in

New Mexico, where combs — especially silver ones — were in great demand.

The historic *Dama de Elche,* a piece of Iberian sculpture excavated in Elche, Spain in 1897, shows a headgear similar to the Spanish tortoise shell comb. In the excavations which have followed in which many remains of Phoenician culture have been found, many combs of metal similar to those in usage today, have been unearthed. See plates 12 and 15.

FASHIONS IN FILIGREE

❦ THE ADORNMENT of the native woman of New Mexico has undergone a varied change since Colonial times, much the same as has the adornment of the women of other countries. There is one kind of adornment, however, that since the beginning of permanent colonization has had little change — filigree jewelry. Filigree jewelry was not the sole adornment of New Mexico women, for jewelry of all kinds, including precious stones, has always been popular with women, regardless of country or race, largely dependent on the woman's station in life. Nor is it to be implied that filigree jewelry is native or common to New Mexico alone. However, due to the degree of perfection that the working of gold filigree reached in New Mexico, and the attachment and esteem in which it was held, we are prompted to claim the working of gold filigree as a craft that is distinctly a New Mexican heritage.

The working of gold and silver into filigree is one of the most ancient of jewelry crafts. The Greeks and Etruscans produced gold and silver filigree of extreme beauty. The natives of India and the Egyptians likewise produced filigree work of note. The round platted chains of fine gold-braided wire with fish hanging from the chain are common to regions of India.

Before the eleventh century, filigree work reached a state of high development in Ireland. During the Middle Ages, Spain, Italy and other European countries developed this art to a finished degree. The Moors of Spain, expert craftsmen in all arts, worked throughout the Peninsula, from where the craft was carried to the Spanish colonies in America.

It is interesting to note that the filigree worker of New Mexico, whether he be working with gold or silver, has always been known as a *platero* or silversmith. It might be that the working of filigree in silver by the Moors, their perfection of it, and its extensive development has caused the name of *plata* (silver) to be identified with the working of filigree in Spanish colonial New Mexico.

Quoting from a census of New Mexico of 1870, we find that the trades in New Mexico at that time were classified into divisions, and the workers were specialists in their fields. Among the list of those engaged in the arts and crafts, we find in this census many *plateros,* yet we know that they worked primarily in gold.

There has been very little working of silver in New Mexico, except the work done by the Indians. Most of the filigree jewelry that has been handed down through the years in New Mexican families has been of gold, with a few hair ornaments and ornamental hair combs in silver.

What is filigree work? Filigree is an ornamental work of fine gold, silver or even copper or brass wire formed into delicate tracery of scrolls, net work and floral designs. The metal threads are twisted, curled, plaited and then united into intricate designs by means of gold or silver solder and borax — until recent times, with the help of the blow pipe. Small grains or *guachaporo* beads of the same metal are then set in the junctions or at intervals to set off the work in finished and beautiful design. This delicate work of scrolls and other designs is protected by a framework of flat wire, thus giving consistency and stability to the piece.

Very little has been written regarding the dress or adornment of the native New Mexico woman since the colonial occupation (other than the information listed in the wills mentioned before). Most information on the subject comes to us through folklore. Ralph E. Twitchell in his volume, *Old Santa Fe,* says, "The women were fond of jewelry and that of native manufacture was admirably fashioned (162)." Josiah Gregg in *Commerce of the Prairies,* in the chapter entitled "Customs and Styles of Dress" condescendingly reaffirms the same account. He says, "Articles of native manufacture, some of which are admirably executed without alloy or counterfeit, are generally preferred."

Wills dating from as early as 1720 name articles of jewelry passed on from one generation to another. The names designated for these articles are identical to those used in New Mexico today. There are earrings of many kinds, *aretes* and *zargillos* (eardrops), *arracadas* (the earring with a pendant), *coquetas* (the long, dangling earrings with jewels), and *pendientes* which may mean eardrops of any kind, as the name implies.

Then there are many styles of necklaces and gold chains. The *bejucos* or rounded braided chains with a fish attached in the manner of the chains mentioned above were similar to those from Peru, and India. There were *cordones* or cords, chains without the fish. The *soguilla* was a flat braided chain with slides of elaborate bead filigree work attached. The *gargantón* or *gargantilla* is the flat necklace with the large brooch-like designs in floral effects. These are rare and typical of New Mexican workmanship. Stones of red and green were sometimes inset.

Rings are mentioned often. There is the *tumbaga*, a wide heavy gold circlet with raised leaves of various hues of gold, either set with stones or with embossed leaves only. The *memoria* is a gold ring in four sections, each part fitting in the other in perfect ensemble. There are leaves of various hues on either side and a stone in the center. (Plate 18). This ring, mostly in silver without a gem, is common to the Orient. There are the plain gold rings set with various stones with floral effects of small stones. These were garnets or rubies of minor value, for the more precious stones have never been common to New Mexico.

In the middle of the 1800's when trade was definitely established with the United States, and also by 1880 when the railroad became an institution in New Mexico, much jewelry other than filigree found its way into New Mexico.

Another ornament graphically named is the *tembladera*.[3] This exquisite hair pin was of silver with a flower at the tip of a spiral causing the flower to tremble with the movement of the head of the wearer. Gold dots in the center of the flower completed a delicate effect.

3 In South America, a *tembladera* is a small, silver dish.

PLATE 17 — *Filigree Jewelry of 1860*

In center, a decorative *Soguilla* or *Gargantón.* Above a small braided chain
with cross. On left, *Bejuco* (gold braided chain with fish),
and on the right, a flat braided watch chain.

There have been many workers of filigree in New Mexico. Workers of note in the 1800's included Rafael Luna (1804-1840), Antonio José Luna (1882-1899), son of Rafael. Antonio taught his sister, Hilaria, who at the age of 60 was still working the craft; although because her sight was failing, her work was not as perfect as in previous years. José Rafael Luna and his nephew, Felipe Guzman, continued the family tradition. These craftsmen were all *vecinos* of Taos, New Mexico. José Rafael moved to Velarde after discontinuing the craft and went into the fruit industry.

Teodoro Lucero, another nephew of José Antonio, and his nephew, Miguel González, worked in Las Vegas for many years, then moved to Socorro and back to Taos.

Juan Antonio Espinosa had a *platería* in Wagon Mound, and lived to be over a hundred years of age.

The Luján's were another family prominent in the history of filigree workers. They worked in New Mexico and southern Colorado, where numerous families of Spanish ancestry lived. Luján made ornaments of gold filigree for the author's mother, Rafaela Martínez de Espinosa, and for her sister, Doña Cirila Martínez de Montoya.

Mrs. Mae Yontz, a widow of a pioneer jeweler in Santa Fe, provided a list of craftsmen who worked for her father-in-law in the late 1800's and early 1900's, among them Cosme Herrera, Willie Salazar, Frank Ortiz (father of Alfredo and Adolfo Ortiz). These brothers had an established jewelry store until late years. Of the above, Adolfo is the only one living. Other filigree workers plying their trade in Santa Fe were Eugenio Sena, a Mr. Labodie and a Mr. Quintana.

In the middle of the 1800's when jewelry stores were few, itinerant craftsmen would go to the various *haciendas,* taking their implements along. Here the fathers of the household would engage them to work their trade, fashioning articles of filigree for the daughters of the household.

Many a former filigree worker whose sight failed was to be seen in the 1900's, on the streets doing menial work.

Needless to say, the attachment which our ancestors had for gold filigree, is still with us, although the working of filigree is only a memory.

PLATE 18 — *Smaller Filigree Jewelry*

The *memoria* is in the lower right hand corner, showing the four sections
separated — they fit together perfectly, each one with a different
design (leaves of various hues and a gem).

THE GORDEJUELA INSPECTION

Prior to Colonization of New Mexico

A REPORT taken from Oñate, colonizer of New Mexico (1595-1628) was published by the Coronado Cuarto Centennial Quivera Society publication, edited by George P. Hammond, University of California and Agapito Rey, University of Indiana. The statement was made by Capitán Conde de Herrera in the Gordejuela Inspection, preparatory to joining the expedition headed by Capitán Juan de Oñate for the purpose of colonizing New Mexico:

Articles of wear to be brought into the region, by his wife Doña Francisca Galindo, his daughter Margarita Conde, his sister-in-law, Doña Geronima Galindo and Anna Galindo:

Nine dresses, two of brown and green cloth, trimmed; another of velvet adorned with velvet belts and gold clasps; another of black satin with silk guimpe; another of black taffeta, trimmed; another of green coarse cloth with sashes embroidered in gold; another of crimson satin, embroidered in gold; another of red satin with sashes and gold trimming; another *(color de arena)* tawny color with white china embroidered skirt; two silk shawls with bead tassels, four pair of thin wool sleeves, one damask and velvet hoop skirt; four ruffs; four gold coiffures; twelve plain bonnets,[4] six shirts, 3 pair fancy cuffs; one necklace of pearls and garnets with large, gold cross; a headdress of pearls with a gold image of Our Lady; some rings set with rubies, two pitchers, a small pot and salt cellar of silver; 6 small and one large spoons, three pair new clogs; eight pairs of slippers, two pairs of high shoes; 3 pairs of stockings of wool and cotton; one bed spread of crimson taffeta trimmed with lace, eight sheets, six pillow cases, three bolsters, two additional pillows embroidered in silk of various colors, two fine woman's hats with gold ribbons, six pairs of gloves; and many other things suitable for the adornment of women and the home."

Captain Cristóbal Vaca lists among personal equipment six suits of coarse cloth and silk for his wife, one dozen shirts, two doublets and two shawls. For his daughters, four sets of cloths

---

4 These bonnets bear no resemblance to those worn by Colonial women in the U.S. They resembled the baby bonnets of today, close-fitting to the head.

cop. 2

for each, thirty-two shirts for his children, and four doublets for each one.

Margarita Conde, daughter of the Captain took four sets of clothing, both wool and silk, besides the linen and foot gear for her personal use.

Doña María de Castellos (sister-in-law) took three complete sets of fancy silk clothes and many other things for her personal use.

Doña Geronima Galindo (sister-in-law) took three complete sets of fancy silk clothes for her own use.

Anna Galindo (sister-in-law) took three sets of clothes, and many other things for her personal use.

The many articles reported by different officials included dozens of cordovan shoes, yards of materials of the following: coarse cloth (jerqueta), Holland linen, Campeche cotton cloth, Chinese silk, Rouen linen, Chinese linen, coarse linen, Simamay cloth (fine piña cloth from the Philippines), pounds of Portuguese thread, yards of frieze, yards of brown cloth, gray cloth, woolen stockings from Brussels, Castilian silk stockings, damask Florentine cloth and many other articles and equipment too numerous to mention.

It would seem that at this period, commerce with the Orient had already been established because of the mention of Chinese silk, Chinese linen, Philippine piña cloth and Chinese embroidery on articles of wear.

The mention of velvet, Florentine damask and gold trimmings indicates the materials used in Europe at this period, also the hats, headdress and shoes. When we read of the dainty elaborate garments that the women going on expeditions to the north of New Spain brought with them, we wonder how adequate were their wardrobes in this strange region where they were to endure the many hardships of colonization.

The women of rank probably fared better than those of common heritage; however, both had to face the discomforts of the elements as well as the animosity of the inhabitants of the region they reached (now New Mexico).

COMMERCE *on the* CHIHUAHUA TRAIL

BY 1808, TRADE CONDITIONS had improved in New Mexico. Evidence of this improvement is shown in the following excerpts from a report submitted by Governor Chacón of New Mexico in 1808 to the Consulate at Vera Cruz:

The natural desire for industry and the needs at hand prompt these inhabitants to exercise the art of weaving wool, shoemaking, tailoring, etc. They weave on narrow combs, *bayetones* (coarse baise), *sargas* (serge), *fresadas* (blankets of wool), *serapes* (rugs), *bayetas* (baize), *sayal* (a coarse woolen stuff) and *gerga* (carpet).

They dye cloth with indigo and brazil-wood, which they bring from outside countries. They also use herbs, with which they are familiar. They apply urine to the herbs. From cotton they weave a *manta*, a corded material closely woven and strong. They use this for stockings and table covers.

Although the government has furnished the weavers with wool, fulling mills and cloth presses, it has not been expedient to bring any of these machines because of the expense, or because of negligence.

Aside from the abundance of wool, there is to be found in the provinces rabbit and squirrel skins of many varieties, beaver pelts, which are used for the making of hats. This art is not carried on extensively because there is no one who has knowledge of it, nor the arts of tanning, curing, belt making and other trades where use is made of pelts and skins.

The external commerce which these provinces carry on once a year with the provinces of Sonora, Viscaya and Coahuila, consists in the selling of oxen, sheep, woolen stuffs, raw wools, some cotton, skins and piñón — the latter very much in demand.

The above named effects are taken in caravans of about 500 men, who are no more than travelers or agents, who leave in the month of November with an escort, and travel together until they reach El Paso, where they separate, about one-third of them go to Sonora, Coahuila and other Presidios. The merchants make their way to Viscaya; some go to the capital of Durango and its environs. The rest remain in Chihuahua, where they exchange their goods for necessities.

The return of the above mentioned caravans is accomplished by bands of horses and mules, and effects to be sold in the province such as cotton of all kinds, cloth of the finest from Querétaro, *bayetas* (woolen cloth), *targas* (silk cloth, printed), *escarlatas* (red cloth), silk, chocolate, sugar, soap, rice, salt, maple sugar, *forro labrado* (printed lining), platina, spices, hats, cured skins and pelts, etc. These effects are not only sufficient for the uses of the province but there are goods left over from year to year.

The trade in the interior is carried on by twelve or fourteen merchants who are not registered and who are not very intelligent in said enterprise. From these there are two or three who direct the others with their own money. That which they manage to bring into the Province, they bring on credit and in that manner they distribute and sell from year to year, from which remittance they have no return on their money except once a year.

They suffer great losses in giving credit, because they generally give credit among the poor and at very reduced prices. It is made more difficult because of the lack of money circulation, which has begun to be used only within the last three years. There are some, especially the Indians, who have no regard for it.

The other inhabitants are nothing more than dealers who are continually exchanging the effects they have at hand, from which a great deal of trouble results in the province. There exists all around, a great deal of malice, deceit and bad faith.

The only instance where formality is effected is in the bartering and that is done with the gentiles (pagans). It is all give and take, and the exchange is carried on by signs. This trade includes cushions, *argueras* (bridles), *macanas* (axes), *fresadas,* indigo, vermillion, mirrors, maple sugar, tobacco, ground corn, corn on the ear, fruit — green and ripe.

In exchange, the gentiles give captives of both sexes, beads, mocassins, wild ponies, pelts of all kinds and buffalo meat. The results of this barter are always favorable to the Spaniards, in one way or other.

The King in his mercy has done his part by exempting the province from customs duties for a period of ten years.

Another proof that the province is not poor, is the fact that there is great luxury in the distribution of internal lands. No families are excepted.

The lack of seeds and vegetables is offset by meats. But there will be a decadence if taxes are levied and no help is given to foster development of industries and arts — and also the development of the metals found in the Province.

Santa Fe, Nuevo Mexico
28 de agosto de 1808

Translated from Archivo No. 1670
Museum of New Mexico — C. G. E.

ACKNOWLEDGEMENTS

To my cousin, Betty Pilkington, for the typing of this manuscript; and for photograph of mantelina.

To my brother, Luis Guillermo, for typing.

To my grand nieces for modeling mantillas and shawls:
Rose Marie Lopez Simms (Mrs. Richard Simms).
Cecily Bryan Kerr, Washington, D.C.

To my niece, Mrs. W. E. Blythe, for modeling her Mantón de Manila.

To Mrs. Max Gonzalez for the photographs of her grandmother, Mrs. Andres Romero.

To Felice Gonzalez for modeling her grandmother's Mantón de Manila.

To my cousin, Mrs. Placida Smith, for the photograph of ermine cape and muff purchased by our grandfather, Captain Julian Espinosa, U.S.A. (Civil War).

To Consuelo Chavez, Santa Fe, for photograph of tortoise shell comb.

To my brother, Gilberto Espinosa, for photograph of Frances Delgado Espinosa in her mother's dress.

To Margaret Delgado (Mrs. Frank V.) Ortiz, for loan of two small filigree brooches for photographing, and family photograph of 1860.

To Cozette Chavez (Mrs. Jack) Lowe, for the loan of filigree watch chain, necklace with guachaporo work on two pairs of filigree earrings for photographing.

BIBLIOGRAPHY

ABERT, LIEUTENANT JAMES WILLIAM. Report to Secretary of War *Examination of New Mexico,* in W. H. Emory, *Notes of Military Reconnoissance.* Washington, 1849. (Senate Document No. 41, 30th Congress).

ANDERSON, RUTH M. *Spanish Costume.* Historical Society of America, 1951.

AGUILER, EMILIANO M. *Trajes Populares de España Vistos por Los Pintores Españoles.* Ediciones Omega, Barcelona, 1948.

ARCHIVES. Museum of New Mexico, Santa Fe.

BARCA, MADAME CALDERON DE LA. *La Vida en México.* Vols. I & II Editorial Porrua, Avenida Republicana 15, México, 1959. Original publication, Boston, 1843.

DALMER, R. *and* JANER SOLER. *Historia del Traje.* Barcelona, 1946.

DAVIS, WILLIAM WATT HART. *El Gringo – New Mexico and Her People.* First Publication, New York, 1857. Reprint, Rio Grande Press, Santa Fe, 1960.

ECHAGUE, J. ORTIZ. *Spain Types and Costumes.* Sociedad General de Publicaciones, Barcelona, 1934.

EVANS, MARY. *Costumes Throughout the Ages.* J. B. Lippincott Co., Philadelphia, 1938.

GREGG, JOSIAH. *Commerce of The Prairies.* New York, 1844.

HAMMOND, GEORGE P. *and* AGAPITO REY. *Don Juan de Oñate Colonizer of New Mexico.* Coronado Cuarto Centennial Publication, University of New Mexico Press, 1953.

BIBLIOGRAPHY

HOHLER, CARL. *History of Costumes.* Dover Publications, 1963.

LAVER, JAMES. *Clothes.* Horizon Press, New York, 1953.

LAVER, JAMES. *Costumes.* London, Hawthorne Books, 1964.

MACKEY, MARGARET *and* LOUISE SOOY. *Early California Costumes.* Stanford Press, Stanford, California, 1932.

PALENCIA, ISABEL DE. *El Traje Regional de España.* Editorial Voluntad, Madrid, 1906.

PARSONS, FRANK. *The Art of Dress.* Doubleday, Doran, New York, 1928.

RANGEL, NICOLAS. *Historia del Toreo en México, Epoca Colonial.* Academia Mexicana de la Historia. Imprenta, Manuel Vellón, Sánchez, México, 1924.

SAGE, ELIZABETH. *Study of Costume Through the Years to Modern Times.* Scribner & Sons, New York, 1926.

SCHWAB, DAVID E. *History of Lace and Embroidery.* Fairchild Publications, Inc., New York, 1951.

TWITCHELL, RALPH E. *Leading Facts of New Mexico History.* Torch Press, Cedar Rapids, Iowa, 1911-12. Reprint, Albuquerque, 1963.

WEBB, WILLIAM H. *Heritage of Dress.* London, 1912.

WILLS. Office of the Cadastral Engineer, Federal Building, Santa Fe, 1714-1830.

WILTON, M. MARGARET. *Annals of Fashion from Earliest Period to Modern Times.* London, 1847.